What People Are Sa...
The Multicultural Church...

"Dan Willis speaks to the heart of the racial challenges that matter in the twenty-first century and provides a real-life blueprint for church leadership. Love is the key! This is a must-read for those who are called to reconciliation by leading multicultural congregations."

—*Pam Morris-Walton*
Host, WVON Gospel Radio
Former event coordinator, City of Chicago
Producer, The Chicago Gospel Music Festival

"If anyone knows the challenges and blessings of a multicultural church, it is my dear friend, Dan Willis. His latest book, *The Multicultural Church*, will begin your journey toward becoming an 'astute observer who can see without prejudice, without preconceptions' and can then minister powerfully to the many diverse cultures in our society. This book will bless and empower your ministry."

—*David Robertson*
Chief operating officer, Inspiration Ministries

"In *The Multicultural Church*, my friend Dan Willis, who started pastoring at the age of sixteen, shares wisdom from his many years of ministry and leadership experience. Learn from his challenges and victories in building a thriving megachurch that is still reaching the hearts and lives of people for Christ all over the world!

—*Steve Munsey*
Senior pastor, Family Christian Center
Munster, IN

THE
MULTICULTURAL
CHURCH

EMBRACING UNITY AND RESTORATION

DAN WILLIS

WHITAKER
HOUSE

THE MULTICULTURAL CHURCH:

Opening Your Doors to Unity and Restoration

www.danwillis.org
www.thelighthousechurch.org
Twitter: http://twitter.com/PastorDanWillis
Facebook: http://facebook.com/lhcanations

ISBN: 978-1-64123-380-4
eBook ISBN: 978-1-64123-381-1
ISBN (special edition hardcover): 978-1-64123-379-8
Printed in the United States of America
© 2019 by Dan Willis

Whitaker House
1030 Hunt Valley Circle
New Kensington, PA 15068
www.whitakerhouse.com

Library of Congress Control Number: 2019951411

1 2 3 4 5 6 7 8 9 10 11 ᴌᴌ 26 25 24 23 22 21 20 19

CONTENTS

INTRODUCTION

Would I do a what?" I said. Quinerra, quintuplets, quinconea…? I couldn't even *say* the word, let alone perform the act of ceremonial leadership it required. However, my ever patient, gracious secretary helped me through not only the correct pronunciation, (it took me three tries to get it right) but explained what a *Quinceañera* is. Armed with a description from the family and a dictionary, she took me to school. A cultural ceremony significant in Hispanic culture, it celebrates the departure from childhood into adulthood. This ceremony is for young girls and takes place when they are fifteen years old.[1] Wow! I felt honored for being asked to fulfill the pastoral aspect of this celebration.

From that first event of Melanis' Quinceañera, more years ago than I can remember, I have been spiritually energized and thrilled with every venture in the very multicultural church aggregate of The Lighthouse Church of all Nations on the south side of Chicago. These exciting and numerous adventures have kept me engaged for over thirty years as pastor. The newness and ever-fresh moments, and the surprises of leading a diverse congregation of cultures, ages, and people long separated by their differences is why leading in this environment is a remarkable journey.

Leadership of this type in Chicago is somewhat unique. The Lighthouse Church blazed the trail for multiculturalism in a city historically known for being the most segregated city in the United States. This fact was documented in a 2008 newspaper article, "Chicago, America's Most Segregated Big City," which appeared in the *Chicago Tribune*. The statistics in this article are alarming. It states that a staggering 84 percent of the black and white population in Chicago need to change neighborhoods in order for the city to be *truly* integrated. The Great Migration of the early twentieth century still carries the impact of real

---

1. *Encyclopedia Britannica*, online edition, *s.v.* "Quinceañera."

estate agents guiding people to specific racially appropriate areas—because Chicagoans are for sure—separate. The separation is deep-seated because it has been ingrained in the landscape of the city for a long time.[2]

In 2008, America enjoyed a historic celebration that changed the face of our United States White House with the election of our forty-fourth president, Barack Obama from Chicago, my hometown! And on January 21, 2013, President Obama was sworn in for a second term. I acknowledged I had given my life, my entire life, to pulling down racial strongholds in Chicago. And though this African American man stood as president, somewhere in the reservoirs of my heart I realized how insignificant, even after thirty years, one man, one church, and one community can be in the face of ugly racism.

I am still pained with the knowledge of how much there is yet to do. How many more walls; how many more conversations; how many more tears; how many more angry people to quiet; how many more misunderstandings; and how many more words like Quinceañera would I yet have to face? Yes, America has made progress on matters of race! But why, for heaven's sake, have politicians and common ordinary men and women once polarized by

2. "Chicago, America's most segregated big city: Racial lines were drawn over the city's history and remain entrenched by people's choice, economics," *Chicago Tribune*, December 26, 2008.

party lines, been the leaders? *Where is the church?* What can we, who are the church, do to become the leaders again and not just be the Johnny-come-lately followers?

America has made progress on matters of race! But why, for heaven's sake, have politicians and common ordinary men and women once polarized by party lines, been the leaders? *Where is the church?* What can we, who are the church, do to become the leaders again and not just be the Johnny-come-lately followers?

The art of bringing harmony to the masses lies in the love all should see in the church of God. In John 13:35, it says, *"This is how everyone will recognize that you are my disciples—when they see the love you have for each other"* (MSG). Here is the difficult question, if America followed the church's example, could segregation and separatism be eliminated? As Christian leaders today, our only option *is* multicultural ministry. If we are not prepared to minister in this growing climate then we are in danger of becoming nonessential to our body of believers.

Jacob Vigdor, of Duke University, summed it up in the aforementioned *Chicago Tribune* article when he said, "What integration requires is the presence of blank slates."[3] However, since this is improbable given how deeply racism is imbedded in the hearts and minds of many, let us look at integration with open minds to fresh ideas, open hearts to change, and open hands to help through this transformation.

> Certainly tradition, housing, and economics played their part in fostering the racial segregation, but we, the church of the living and loving God, we too have our part in this situation. We are the salt of the earth. We are the head and not the tail. We are the leaven that can cause attitudes to rise above the status quo. We are the leaders God is using today.

Certainly tradition, housing, and economics played their part in fostering the racial segregation, but we, the church of the living and loving God, we too have our part in this situation. We are the salt of the earth. We are the head and not the tail. We are the leaven that can cause attitudes to rise above the status quo. We are the leaders God is using today. Biblical heroes such as Paul, Barnabas, Mary, Esther, Moses, Aaron, and many others are long gone. However, their example remains. God has put this *treasure* in earthen vessels (see 2 Corinthians 4:7)—*in our*

<hr>

3. Ibid.

generation. This means no one is exempt. This great learning project will never be ordinary or business as usual. And it starts where we are right now, in our living rooms—in our homes. If we do not know how to take care of our own homes, then how can we take care of God's church? (See 1 Timothy 3:5.) The Bible says we have many teachers but not many fathers. (See 1 Corinthians 4:15.)

Racial change and reconciliation start at home. Not on television, not at school, and not even at church, but at home. And don't be afraid to mess up along the way. Just get up and start again. Have fun! We fear human failure or that being transparent will discredit God, so we just bide our time and keep doing the same thing. Come on—try! Dance a little! Yes, you will trip but you will be so loved for trying to dance.

In the pages of this book, I will share with you a few things to help you successfully minister in a diverse culture. Some successes are brought to fruition by being uncomfortable. Even if some of the lessons are learned by tripping in the dance, I am on my feet and holding out my hand, inviting you to the dance floor! Come on—*dance*—try this; it will change your life! Lighten up your feet, and let's bring our church into the fullness of joy that heaven will be. Because remember—there is no back of the bus in heaven. We are going to a place where those who arrive have been made *one* by the blood of Jesus. (See Galatians 3:28.)

We are all God's chosen carriers of fairness, justice, truth, compassion, and honor. We cannot fail. We must get this into the hearts of our children and their children before we go. And, YES WE CAN!

1

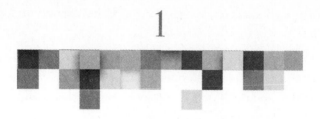

THE BEGINNING

I remember feeling awful as a six or seven-year-old child, hearing relatives who claimed to be saved use disparaging terms for people of other races. I remember thinking they were unkind and stupid. Little did I realize I was being prepared, even at this early age, for a ministry that would begin in full force at the age of sixteen.

At that time, racial discussions hovered around black and white issues. During my preteen and adolescent years, we were at the height of the Civil Rights Movement. It was a sensitive time in Chicago and in America. Four little girls were the victims of a hateful racially motivated bombing in September 1963. President John F. Kennedy was assassinated two months later in November. Malcolm X was assassinated in February 1965. Civil Rights leader Martin Luther King Jr. was assassinated in April 1968. Senator Robert Kennedy was assassinated two months later. So I felt I had no time to waste.

For me, tearing down the barriers started with music. God in his infinite wisdom uses music as a powerful bonding agent. It is a tool to bring the saints together.

My parents often hosted preachers, evangelists, singing groups, and relatives in our home. I was ecstatic because I knew the byproduct of these visits would be an outing to at least one or maybe even two churches.

Blessed are the memories of my mother and father taking us to hear gospel music at churches around the city. We went to Bethlehem Healing Temple at 14 S. Oakley Boulevard in Chicago to hear Evangelist Mattie B. "Mother" Poole on Sunday afternoons. Mother Poole was the epitome of a woman of God, faith being her most profound gift. She healed the sick, she loved children, and she was a gifted musician. The legacy of Mother Poole lives today in the hearts of many. I wish everyone could have heard Mother Poole. Oh my! What preaching! What joy! And, oh my, what music! Then on to the First Church of Deliverance at 43rd and Wabash for the 11:00 P.M. Sunday night live broadcast. The choir was indescribable! And so it was that these churches shaped me. I could never settle for normal again. I craved this anointing, I craved this energy, and I craved the love I felt from the congregations when they saw me loving this experience.

Music is a gift and a tool I believe God wants us to use to its full potential. Consider David and King Saul. Saul lost his fellowship with God because of his disobedience. (See 1 Samuel 15:24–26.) God's spirit departed from King Saul. An evil spirit sent by God tormented him, and he needed relief. David ministered to King Saul with music, specifically with the harp. This gave King Saul reprieve from the demons God sent to him, (See 1 Samuel 16:14, 23.) David's music quieted the soul of King Saul.

Shall we not consider the powerful potential of music, which has ability to make demons flee? Tami Briggs, therapeutic harpist in Minnesota, notes, "The harp is a perfect instrument for relaxation—it naturally soothes and comforts and moves people to their peaceful core. This is a sacred moment when healing happens."[4] Music—transcending racial wounds and scars, how awesome and potent is that? This influence of music is some of what I felt when I heard the different melodies of a music genre I was unfamiliar with as a young man. I may not have

4. Briggs, Tami, "Music's Unspoken Messages," *Creative Nursing*, October, 2011.

known what the philosophical impact would be in my life, but something was changing in my soul.

In the twentieth and twenty-first centuries, music in a clinical environment is recognized as a therapy for mental illness. Music in operating rooms has been documented to speed recovery, stabilize blood pressure, and have a calming effect on patients. Music therapy is used for terminally ill cancer patients to bring peace and calm to both the patients and their families. Music therapy is used to treat sleep disorders. The type of music typically used is classical music. Mozart seems to be a favored composer.[5] Therefore, it is conceivable that the church would take the natural components of the healing power of music and use it to usher in the spirit of oneness among believers. Music acts as a catalyst to bring together all races in America and abroad. Music was and remains a critical component of unity within God's body of believers.

> Music acts as a catalyst to bring together all races in America and abroad. Music was and remains a critical component of unity within God's body of believers.

As musical director and founder of the Pentecostals of Chicago, a culturally diverse group of singers representing

---

5. Ibid.

what we believe heaven will look like, we take our message of unity to the streets of Chicago, the nation, and the world. At the heart of music is its healing power. While effective for those with physical and mental ailments, music's power is also used to transcend the heart, healing those old wounds of racism and prejudices. The power to reconcile through music is at our fingertips. We need only to use it. We are fully equipped. (See 2 Timothy 3:17.)

Through music we can bridge the gap to reconcile the masses. I understand that God called me to bridge the gap with love. I am on a mission to bring the races together. I know that God has assigned this task to me. Am I the only one? Certainly not. Thankfully, many share this assignment with me. Once while laboring with the idea of uniting God's church, I wrote the song, "Bridging the Gap" and would like to share the lyrics with you.

> *"Bridging the Gap"*
> *So glad you came into our lives*
> *You showed us that there's no black or white*
> *Love has no color, it's plain to see*
> *Now there's a task that's not so hard*
> *But we all must do our part to live peacefully*
> *Now there's a job for us to do*
> *Yes, that includes me and you*
> *Hand in hand together will get it done—I'm a believer!*
> *Count on me right from the start*

I'll take the first step, yes, I'll do my part
Let's let love ring from our hearts
We're bridging the gap–for one and all
I'm calling one and all
Let's stand in the gap—hear the Spirit call
Somebody stand tall
What a bridge we all can build—together—all who
will
Now the choice is yours
There's a world, hear them cry
Let's just show them that we care
And unite and unite!
Bridging the gap—we won't sit still
Stand in the gap—if we don't who will?

God has made our bodies with internal rhythmic melodies. Ellen F. Franklin points this out in her article in *Massage Magazine*. "Within the body, there are biological rhythms that govern organic life. Lungs dilate and contract every three seconds; the heart beats seventy times per minute; the stomach contracts three times per minute; the ovaries release an egg every twenty-eight days; the life span of red corpuscles is 128 days. Every organ, bone and tissue in the body has its own resonant frequency."[6] The fact that the body is a symphony in and of itself,

---

6. Franklin, Ellen F. "Vibrational Healing—The Therapeutic Use of Sound and Music," *Massage Magazine*, July, 2012, 42–47.

and the concept that, "through resonance, it is possible for the vibrations of one body to reach out and touch or activate another body"[7] is mind blowing! This observation supports the spiritual influence of music when it travels throughout the entire body of Christ.

Have you ever been in a service when God is ministering through a minstrel in song and the essence of that song leaps from one believer to the next? This phenomenon is called *entrainment*. It also occurs in clinical music therapy. Briggs, while playing the harp, soothed a patient who struggled with restlessness the entire day and was unable to be calmed even though he had received medication. The low, soothing voice of his wife did not help. Briggs administered calm to him through music therapy. She "started playing a song that was a bit agitated. The next song was slower. After the first couple of songs, it became apparent that the music was distracting him enough to be less fidgety. Each musical selection thereafter was slower and s-l-o-w-e-r, until the music barely pulsed. He was getting sleepy and within twenty minutes, he was peacefully asleep."[8]

Franklin states, "Not all sounds [music] are pleasing; some discordant sounds can be used to break up stagnation in the body, clear energetic blockages and reduce scar

---

7. Ibid.
8. Ibid, Briggs.

tissue."[9] This is a powerful analogy. Apply that to a song that hits right at the heart of an obstacle in your life. As you listen to it, you begin to relate to the words or perhaps just the beat and rhythm stirs something in your soul. Spiritual stumbling blocks are being removed, unforgiveness is released, and the healing begins. Praise God for the wisdom of making music part of our DNA!

I remember a story from a member of my church regarding her response to a question while on a job interview for a high-performing managerial position. Her prospective employer wanted to know how she would deal with potential job-related crises. The interviewer asked, "How do you calm yourself in stressful situations?" She answered, "I always turn to music. Without fail, music destresses me within a few minutes and calms my spirit." Without a moment's hesitation, she immediately drew on her love of music as a calming remedy for difficult situations.

How could I bring everyone together? It was an idea so lofty I relegated it to others who were older and famous but God was preparing *my* tender heart! Praise God! (See Proverbs 22:6.) God knew that these experiences, the music and the anointing, would help me to understand other cultures and that this knowledge would later be instrumental in helping me lead a multicultural

---

9. Ibid, Franklin.

congregation. Hallelujah! All I knew is I wanted everyone to enjoy this treat. However, this was only a small part of the gigantic picture God was beginning to paint on the canvas of my life.

God knew that these experiences, the music and the anointing, would help me to understand other cultures and that this knowledge would later be instrumental in helping me lead a multicultural congregation.

I never dreamed I could have a part, albeit a small part, in leading this journey to reconciliation. I believed in and aspired to helping a church when I was old enough. But to *lead* a congregation into a multicultural community of believers? It never crossed my mind. But then again, we know that God chooses the foolish things of this world to confound the wise. (See 1 Corinthians 1:27.)

How would I do this? I knew the church had to be the leader if these walls were coming down. I knew I had to lead the charge from right where I was. I began to look for instructions on how to lead the type of church I knew God wanted me to form. But the more I looked for printed help, the less I found. Most of what I learned came from trial and error. The lessons began when I found myself, a tenderhearted sixteen-year-old, "accidentally" pastoring a church in Chicago of about fifteen people, and continue pastoring to this day. We now have the largest multicultural congregation in Chicago's South Side, representing sixty-seven nations (wow!) with over two thousand members. During these decades, I experienced so much failure, tears, joy, and excitement, and did a lot of listening! The door to the clueless is open. Wanna come in?

2

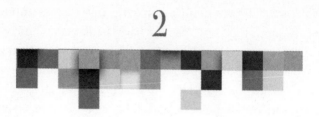

RECONCILIATION

The Scripture in 2 Corinthians 5:18–20 places us in full-time ministry.

> But all things are from God, Who through Jesus Christ reconciled us to Himself [received us into favor, brought us into harmony with Himself] and gave to us the ministry of reconciliation [that by word and deed we might aim to bring others into harmony with Him]. It was God [personally present] in Christ, reconciling and restoring the world to favor

with Himself, not counting up and holding against [men] their trespasses [but cancelling them], and committing to us the message of reconciliation (of the restoration to favor). So we are Christ's ambassadors, God making His appeal as it were through us. We [as Christ's personal representatives] beg you for His sake to lay hold of the divine favor [now offered you] and be reconciled to God. (AMPC)

This is the ministry of reconciliation, to heal the many wounds caused by segregation and separatism. That other job we do from nine to five, Monday through Friday, is our side job. If we are going to chisel away at this decay in our church, we have to realize that we are in full-time ministry, reconciling God's people to a Savior who said, *"There is neither Jew nor Greek, slave nor free, male nor female, for you are all one in Christ Jesus* (Galatians 3:28 BSB). Now that is color blind! You are the one chosen by God for this great joy.

Change is one of the most difficult things to do. In fact, I think when we hear the word or the idea of change, either we embrace it, or run from it as far as we can. But our relationship with God was changed through the blood of Jesus Christ.

The Greek word for reconciliation is *katallasso*, or the root word *allasso*. Both words mean "to change." Reconciliation is a change from enmity to friendship.[10] For me, the word *change* is powerful. Change is one of the most difficult things to do. In fact, I think when we hear the word or the idea of change, either we embrace it, or run from it as far as we can. But our relationship with God was changed through the blood of Jesus Christ. In positioning my ministry for reconciliation, the process began with me. I was the catalyst who got this whole party started.

One thing is certain. It is not about just me. Changing the hearts of God's people is a spiritual matter that is to be handled with care. I can't say that I sat down and mapped out the plan that would carry to fruition my desire to bring different cultures together. But God had the plan for me. The steps of a righteous man are ordered by the Lord. (See Psalm 37:23.)

I remember as a child seeing television shows and reading comic books about heroes and superheroes. Most of the time these guys did not work alone. Generally, they had someone they could trust to help them with their good deeds: to save a lady in distress, catch the bad guys, and keep aliens from conquering the world. These dependable

---

10. Easton, M. G. "Reconciliation," *Illustrated Bible Dictionary* 3rd ed. Nashville: Thomas Nelson, 1897.

characters are known as sidekicks. Dr. Leonard Smith wrote an article in *Gospel Today* magazine elaborating on the attributes of a sidekick: they will not upstage or outshine the hero; they are trusted companions; and they are comfortable being in the role of either a subordinate, or a partner. However, Dr. Smith offered his personal definition of a sidekick. He said, "A sidekick is an individual who proudly views himself as a subordinate and faithfully supports and collaborates with a person in a superior position." Dr. Smith went on to say that the idea of a sidekick is also an excellent "Kingdom Principle."[11]

I applaud Dr. Smith's interpretation of a sidekick and his thought process of its use in kingdom building. I have found when operating in the ministry of reconciliation, sidekicks are an absolute necessity. A successful sidekick from a ministerial standpoint translates into my vision of one hundred "middle-door pastors" for the Lighthouse Church. Developing these pastors means that they stand *with me* and stand *in for me*. These pastors continue to blaze the idea and concept of reconciliation by the blood of Jesus Christ. They are ambassadors for Christ, and in turn teach others to do the same. This is how the chain of prejudice is broken.

---

11. Smith, Leonard, "The Power of a Sidekick," *Gospel Today*, August, 2009, 46–48.

As I mentioned earlier, I drew the roadmap to this ministry as I was going. I made a few, maybe more than a few, mishaps along the way, but I allowed God to do what only He can do. I stepped aside and said, "God, it's your party!" This party developed into over eighty different ministries at the Lighthouse Church. Some of these ministries are expressions of different ethnicities, similar to my conducting a Quinceañera.

In Jesus' ministry to the broken and lost, He came to them just as they were. He put himself in their place so He could effectively bring the message of salvation. The way to save the lost, as well as fuse together hearts broken by misunderstandings, misconceptions, and mistakes is to minister wearing a blindfold.

In Jesus' ministry to the broken and lost, He came to them just as they were. He put himself in their place so He could effectively bring the message of salvation. The way to save the lost, as well as fuse together hearts broken by misunderstandings, misconceptions, and mistakes is to minister wearing a blindfold. When I say that, I do not mean to be literally blindfolded, but to be blind to the exterior person and only concerned with the interior person. I come to my congregation naked (not on the outside), and they see me just as I am. I think this is critical because when ministering to different ethnicities, they can spot a fake a mile away. A fake is turned off like a faucet, and anything said falls on deaf ears. Make people feel as though they are the most important persons in the world when you are talking to them. Never talk *at* anyone, and never assume anything.

As a young pastor with a heart to reconcile the masses and without any written guideline or manual available, I had the ultimate authority for direction. I believe in several basic principles: *acceptance*, *patience*, and *empathy*. Along with these principles, I incorporated the fruit of the Spirit described in Galatians 5:22–23:

> *But the fruit of the [Holy] Spirit [the work which His presence within accomplishes] is love, joy (gladness), peace, patience (an even temper, forbearance), kindness, goodness (benevolence), faithfulness, Gentleness (meekness, humility), self-control (self-restraint, continence).* (AMPC)

Operating under these influences will bring no charge against you. No one will have anything negative to say. These are simple guidelines, but not always simple to emulate. They continue to be a work-in-progress in the body of believers, and *me*, even today.

Jesus said,

You shall love the Lord your God with all your heart and with all your soul and with all your mind (intellect). This is the great (most important, principal) and first commandment. And a second is like it: You shall love your neighbor as [you do] yourself. These two commandments sum up and upon them depend all the Law and the Prophets.

(Matthew 22: 37–40 AMPC)

I feel that these are often-assumed commandments. We all take for granted that to admonish or reinforce this direct instruction from Jesus should go without saying. We further assume this commandment is a *given*, and everyone does it second-nature. However, leading in a multicultural capacity makes this a critical component of reconciliation. Without love, reconciliation is impossible. Because of the uncompromising love of God, He gave His Son, Jesus, to show us the way to reconciliation.

The journey continues. With reconciliation comes an understanding of what is happening in our society. What is the political climate? What is occurring outside the church walls impacting your congregation? The apostle James instructs that if someone is hungry, feed them. (See James 2:15–16.) Sometimes you must be prepared to meet the physical need *before* you can minister to the soul. In meeting the need, try to discern what he or she hungers for. Sometimes it is not only food, but a loving word, a listening ear, or a kind voice. Ministry is to the whole person.

With reconciliation comes an understanding of what is happening in our society. What is the political climate? What is occurring outside the church walls impacting your congregation? The apostle James instructs that if someone is hungry, feed them. Sometimes you must be prepared to meet the physical need *before* you can minister to the soul.

In addition, find out about the customs and the culture of your congregation. Ignorance in this case is not bliss. This is not to say that you will incorporate every custom or tradition, as that may not be of God. But it provides a point of reference when you are counselling a member.

3

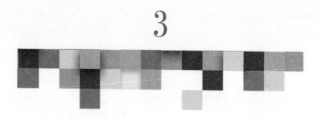

WOVEN TOGETHER:
RECONCILIATION THROUGH
UNCONDITIONAL ACCEPTANCE

Acceptance is the willingness to receive from others. This can be an apology, a gift, love, or affection which encompasses both the intangible and tangible. For me, acceptance is to unconditionally receive someone without outside prejudice or influences. God accepted you and me before we were even thought of. *"Before I formed thee in the belly I knew thee; and before thou camest forth out of the womb I sanctified thee"* (Jeremiah 1:5). Before Momma and Daddy ever met, God accepted you without regard of your hair color, your eye color, or your skin color. He did not care how you walked, or talked, or what country, city, or state you came from. What He did do was accept you unconditionally because He loved you. He calls us to do same.

In the fifteenth chapter of John, Jesus talks about our being branches of the true vine. He tells us that His Father, the Gardener, will take care of the vine. If one of the branches does not produce fruit, He removes that branch, so the other branches remain healthy. The Gardener only prunes branches that produce fruit so they will produce even more fruit. He does this as long the branches remain part of the vine.

We are, of course, the branches. As long as we are attached to the vine we remain in Christ's love. His love is so unique and has such depth that it raises the level of the branches from servants, to friends. *"Greater love has no one than this: to lay down one's life for one's friends…. I no longer call you servants…. Instead, I have called you friends"* (John 15:13, 15 NIV). Awesome!

This takes me right to Romans 12:5 which states, *"So in Christ we, though many, form one body, and each member belongs to all the others"* (NIV). Once the concept of friendship is understood to coincide with oneness, we can readily accept each other just as we are. It is not that we don't *see* each other's differences. We are all uniquely and wonderfully made. But we need to accept these differences without thinking that we need to categorize these differences and act upon them.

Once the concept of friendship is understood to coincide with oneness, we can readily accept each other just as we are. It is not that we don't *see* each other's differences. We are all uniquely and wonderfully made. But we need to accept these differences without thinking that we need to categorize these differences and act upon them.

God has laid out the plan and the roadmap for successful acceptance. (See James 2:1–4 and 1 Samuel 16:7.) He teaches that the outside appearance is irrelevant. Unconditional acceptance is a heart matter. Only God is equipped to change the internal heart.

At Lighthouse Church over the years, not only have many different ethnic groups graced our threshold, but also people with different religious influences. Each person brought their own religious history: the Church of God in Christ (COGIC); Missionary Baptist; Catholic; Methodist; Pentecostal; (this list is not exhaustive), in addition to the unsaved and the unchurched. But what a wonderful opportunity to have a body of believers that reflect such diversity! This is why I fell that being a nondenominational congregation is critical in order to be effective in multicultural ministry.

As the overseer, I was open to what the religious histories of my church family could bring to the table for the ministry of Lighthouse Church. It is great seeing the traditional exuberance and hearing loud praise from those with COGIC backgrounds being adopted by those who came from a quieter method of worship. And watching some of these changes come to fruition, well, God does have a since of humor! And if I am laughing, I am sure Jesus is having fun too. But this is one of the ways that acceptance occurs naturally. It was never orchestrated. You also see *acceptance* in the songs chosen for praise and worship on Sunday mornings. There are no black, white, Hispanic, or Asian praise songs, just God praise songs. What a blessing to the body of Christ.

Acceptance became a byproduct of this diversity. Was acceptance an overnight success? No, it continues to be a work-in-progress. I admit, I muddled through this. I operated in a reactive mode rather than a proactive mode. But we serve an awesome Savior, and when we put the puzzle pieces together haphazardly, God comes in and makes sense out of what appeared to be nonsense. I had hoped everyone would grow at the same pace, but, of course, that did not happen. We work at it even when the progress is slow. Change is difficult. But with acceptance comes common ground and connection. God knows we are not really that different. He simply asks us to understand each other.

Change is difficult. But with acceptance comes common ground and connection. God knows we are not really that different. He simply asks us to understand each other.

Reconciliation through unconditional acceptance: practice it until you get it right. Acceptance is trained and acquired behavior. If you feel uncomfortable initially—that's great! Try visiting other churches in different neighborhoods. Please don't only go to familiar churches or to the restaurants you frequently patronize. Acceptance is something practiced as you go about living. This may seem simplistic. While it is simple to say, it is not as simple to do.

4

A HEART FOR PATIENCE

Me and patience. What a task! For someone impatient by nature, (just ask my wife and my mother) this was a lesson I had to repeat several times. In fact, every once in a while I still need to bring it under subjection–LOL! So many times as a new pastor, patience was a tool I used over and over. As I waited for the "lightbulb" to come on for many in my congregation, I learned lessons of patience.

The journey of reconciliation requires patience. Reconciliation is a process, and different people move at different paces. I had to be cognizant of the different levels of spiritual acceptance and growth in my church family. I knew we were all brothers and sisters, but we still had far to go in learning to deal with one another and accept change. God not only dealt with me regarding patience, but He also helped me teach this principle to the sheep He had so graciously blessed me to lead. As this attribute became evident in my life, I am thankful that patience begets patience.

As a leader or a lay person in the ministry of uniting people in a diverse body of believers, renewing your strength (physical, mental, and emotional) is critical to stay hopeful and believe that the people of God under your leadership will embrace oneness in the body of Christ.

Why is patience important in multicultural ministry? Why even add this to one of the principles of an effective urban ministry? Well, *"They that wait upon the* Lord *shall renew their strength; they shall mount up with wings as eagles; they shall run, and not be weary; and they shall walk, and not faint"* (Isaiah 40:31). As a leader or a lay person in the ministry of uniting people in a diverse body of believers, renewing your strength (physical, mental, and emotional) is critical to stay hopeful and believe that the people of God under your leadership will embrace oneness in the body of Christ. Eagles are powerful birds. God provides us a supernatural power so that in times of hardship and struggle, spiritually and physically, we are able to move forward with His agenda, and not become worn out or fall from exhaustion, as we carry out His plan for ministry.

The focus of multicultural ministry, which in many cases is urban ministry, is to be a reconciler across a diverse body of believers. It is an overwhelming task if you think about it, but I don't believe I ever did—I simply endeavored to do it. In a city like Chicago, even though the first African American mayor, the late Mayor Harold Washington, was elected in 1983, the city was still primarily segregated. Some areas of the city suffered from white flight as many whites moved into several suburban areas. To substantiate the racial climate in Chicago, I would like to quote an article from the *New York Times* written right before the mayoral election in 1983.

> But as Chicago marks its 150th birthday this year, there are many underlying problems. There are the stark divisions between whites and blacks, possibly the most dramatic of any major American city. There is the continued drain of families to the increasingly independent suburbs, which for the first time have more residents than the city they surround on three sides. Jobs Lost as Factories Leave. . .

The population, down from its 3.6 million peak in 1960, has become 40 percent black and 14 percent Hispanic, with one out of five Chicagoans living in poverty. Analysis of new census data shows that fully 43 percent of the county's black households have but one adult, a woman, compared with 13 percent in white homes.

The races generally co-exist in separate neighborhoods, but rarely do they mix, and city services do not perform uniformly for all races.

"Our city," said James Compton, president of the Urban League, "has carried the stigma of being America's most segregated city for far too long."[12]

I am endeavoring to paint a picture of the racial climate of Chicago in the early eighties, when my ministry was in its infancy. Another article in the *New York Times* comments on a report presented by independent consultants as to whether or not inroads had been made in Chicago regarding desegregation.

The report is replete with comments such as, "little change occurred in segregation between 1980 and 1982." The consultants said that the

12. Malcolm, Andrew H., "Chicago Primary Marked by Candidates as Diverse as the City," *New York Times*, February 22, 1983.

city not only had failed to move quickly to carry out its voluntary desegregation plan under a court settlement with the Justice Department, but asserted that the plan itself was inadequate to end decades of racial separation in the nation's most segregated city.

They noted that while some progress had been made, 82 percent of Chicago's black elementary students were in schools without a single white student, and a sixth of all Hispanic students were in overcrowded, racially isolated schools.[13]

Wow! What a task God had set before me. But, is there anything too hard for God? *"Now faith is the substance of things hoped for, the evidence of things not seen"* (Hebrews 11:1). In my spirit I retained this blessed assurance that what I envisioned, a body of believers without respect of person, would come to pass in my lifetime. As I continued to dance, many dancers came along with me. It happened at just the right time. Of course, I wanted success overnight, but that only happens in Hollywood. Often I went into my closet and wept over the injustices I saw in this great city I loved. I craved love among the people of God. My heart was heavy that God's people continued to worship on Sunday in predominately segregated churches. But,

---

13. "Chicago Faulted on Desegregation," *New York Times*, July 11, 1983.

> *If my people, which are called by my name, shall humble themselves, and pray, and seek my face, and turn from their wicked ways; then will I hear from heaven, and will forgive their sin, and will heal their land.* (2 Chronicles 7:14)

I believed and waited patiently for the healing to come forth. It happened one member at a time. Hallelujah! Multicultural and urban ministry is unique. Everyone may not be called to proceed in this type of ministry. However, if God has called you for this, He will equip you for it. You will succeed in due season if you just don't faint.

My heart leaped each Sunday when I saw people from all walks of life claiming Lighthouse Church as home. Diversity in ministry encompasses more than ministering to diverse culture, but also to people of different ages and backgrounds. I was challenged to minister on many different levels. It kept me constantly experimenting with new dance steps, and I am here to tell you that I often stumbled, but God had compassion on me and helped me to understand those I partnered with in the dance.

5

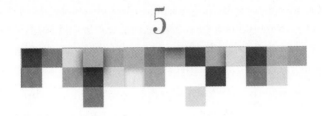

BECOMING ONE

I could focus on the need for compassion, sympathy, and understanding, but since the word *empathy* covers all of these attributes, this is the third principle to discuss as we pursue this journey of reconciliation. I don't believe that we have a better example of empathy than that of our Lord and Savior Jesus Christ. He died for us! *"For God so loved the world that he gave his only begotten Son, that whosoever believeth in him should not perish, but have everlasting life"* (John 3:16). Why did He die? Because He wants us to live! We were spiritually dead because of sin. The blood

of animals was no longer sufficient to purchase our salvation. We could only be redeemed by untainted blood. This
truth transcends religion and race. It is God saying, "I love
you unconditionally." Isn't that awesome?

I pray that my love for people would be unconditional
and uncompromising. I do not want to emulate contingent
love or reciprocal love. The example of Christ's empathy
only reinforces in my mind the need for abiding compassion, the willingness to work toward understanding, and
the need to always be ready with a sympathetic ear. As
the shepherd of a growing body of diverse believers, it is
my goal to try and relate to their backgrounds, to care
about where they have been, and to care about where they
need to go. Healing is universal. I know that only God
through his abiding Holy Spirit can heal old wounds carried throughout generations of hardship and abuse. Oh,
my God, my eyes are tearing up as I write this!

As the shepherd of a growing body of diverse believers, it
is my goal to try and relate to their backgrounds, to care
about where they have been, and to care about where
they need to go. Healing is universal. I know that only
God through his abiding Holy Spirit can heal old wounds
carried throughout generations of hardship and abuse.

In America, if you go back far enough, people who were not from Britain or not Anglo-Saxon, a word not commonly used today, were mistreated. Britain is a class-based society, and some of its prejudices came with the British to the New World centuries ago.

Today in the twenty-first century, discrimination still exists against immigrants from certain countries. People from Mexico and the continent of Africa are examples. Every minority ethnic group in America suffers from some type of discrimination. High on the list are Hispanics and African Americans. Hispanics now outnumber African Americans as the largest minority, representing just over eighteen percent as of 2017.[14] Along with this majority status for Hispanics is the perception that many are illegal immigrants. This causes a perception that Hispanics are taking away the jobs and resources of U.S. citizens. Hispanics have also brought to America their own set of customs and traditions. Though the bias against Hispanics may not be always evident, it is something that those of this heritage deal with every day in this society.

As I think about discrimination, I ask myself, *What does this really mean, and how does it effect this*

14. U.S. Bureau of the Census, *Annual Estimates of the Resident Population by Sex, Age, Race, and Hispanic Origin for the United States and States: April 1, 2010 to July 1, 2017*, prepared by the Population Division, Bureau of the Census, Washington, D.C., 2018.

population of awesome people that God has placed before me? Discrimination is when people are denied rights and judged unfairly because of how they look, where they were born, or their social position. It is senseless and has no valid reason for existing. The idea that a person's equal rights or opportunities are contingent upon circumstances completely out of their control is ungodly. Adding to this tragedy, some use the Word of God to support their selfish agenda.

People who were once called Colored, Negro, Black, and now African American have suffered in this country more than any other minority group. Unlike other minorities, most African Americans were brought here under horrific conditions known as the middle passage, and were forced into a form of slavery few other human beings had ever endured or experienced. Even though slavery ended over one hundred and fifty years ago, the repercussions are still evident in almost every area of this generation. This does not discount the huge accomplishments that have been attained, including our first African American president, Barack Obama. But it is in order to say there is still much to do. I pray for the forgiveness of America's slavery-enabling ancestors. They need forgiveness so that today's generation can receive healing in Jesus' name. Forgiveness is a critical component for enabling those wounded in America's past to move on.

I pray for the forgiveness of America's slavery-enabling ancestors. They need forgiveness so that today's generation can receive healing in Jesus' name. Forgiveness is a critical component for enabling those wounded in America's past to move on.

In addition to understanding racial discrimination, one must also look at the poor in this country. They have definitely been an underserved population. Their plight, sometimes brought on by generational poverty and despair, must be met with great empathy and compassion. Had it not been for the goodness of the Lord, where would we be? Poverty has touched every family in America, either directly or indirectly. If you are not poor, you certainly have a relative, friend, or someone you know who is.

The list goes on. Working with a diverse group of people demands that as a leader you make an attempt to walk in their shoes. The Bible admonishes us to do this when it instructs us to bear each other's burdens. (See Galatians 6:2.) In order to feel a person's hardship, sorrow, or pain you need to have some idea of what they are. Many times we want to avoid the unpleasantries of life and pretend they don't exist because they may not be a part of the environment in which we live.

However, people have histories, and along with many histories come trauma, abuse, and suffering. I physically cannot become Hispanic or African American but I can empathize with some of the emotional hardships they have endured in a society that has not always embraced their uniqueness and culture. Critical to the ministry of multiculturalism is to understand the lives of your members. How? By living among them. Ministry does not begin and end on Sundays. It is an ongoing process.

people have histories, and along with many histories come trauma, abuse, and suffering. I physically cannot become Hispanic or African American but I can empathize with some of the emotional hardships they have endured in a society that has not always embraced their uniqueness and culture. Critical to the ministry of multiculturalism is to understand the lives of your members.

Look at Jesus and Zacchaeus, the tax collector. (See Luke 19:2–5.) Jesus did not just speak with him about salvation, He also showed him by sitting down and eating with Zacchaeus and his family. Jesus could have bypassed the woman at the well. (See John 4.) She is a Samaritan, living with a man she is not married to, and has been married five times. But Jesus comes to the well purposely so He can meet her where she is—physically, emotionally, and spiritually.

To carry the mantle of empathy, we must dig deep. We may not want to, but we need to. Endeavoring to understand a person's experience goes beyond being nice and tolerant. To be empathetic helps you feel your brother and sister's pain, and also joy. My goal is to bring the gospel, the good news, in a way that is relevant today, to let the injured know there is healing in the Balm of Gilead.

6

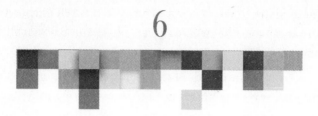

TOLERANCE

Is tolerance necessary to incorporate into the journey of reconciliation? The attribute of acceptance, which we covered earlier, appears to be a close relative of tolerance. But with tolerance, I have to be careful of how far I go. Ushering in complete tolerance may be too broad, especially when tolerance encompasses ideologies which may not fall under biblical doctrine.

Several synonyms for tolerance include lenience, open-mindedness, broad-mindedness, and easiness. Keeping these attributes in mind, I had to be careful of what these meant when it came to their implementation within the body of Christ. Different denominations crossed the threshold of Lighthouse Church, bringing with them some good, and some not-so-good traditions and ideologies. If they were unbiblical, then I had no choice except to say, "Whoa now!" Just because Lighthouse Church is nondenominational does not mean anything goes. I am also sure there are a few differences of opinion on that.

A former Catholic can confess their sin to me if they want, but I let them know that only God has the power to forgive. Church of God in Christ (COGIC) folks bring with them convocations, invocations, and ramifications, but these types of programs, though great for COGIC, were not what God gave me to do at Lighthouse. My calling was to teach another way. It was to find common ground, to instruct and labor with those unaccustomed to reaching out directly to God our Father with cries of repentance, and help them accept forgiveness already provided by the precious blood of Jesus. Programs are for our glory. I did not want anything to outshine the simple message that Jesus saves.

In my mind, tolerance almost has a negative connotation. Tolerance is restricted by time. You only deal with it for short periods. It is not about embracing the differences. It is pretending to be comfortable worshipping or living in a diverse culture. Tolerance alone does not bring about a change of heart. As a believer, you cannot be open to anything and everything. You must be mindful of what you put in your spirit and mind. It is not what is outside of a man that defiles him. It is what is inside him. (See Mark 7:15.)

7

ARE YOU GETTING ENOUGH FRUIT?

I love tangerines. They are delicious, and so much easier to peel than oranges. The skin is thinner, and they make less of a mess than oranges. When I eat my tangerine, I make a production out of it. I love taking the time to savor each section slowly so I can enjoy it as long as possible. Not all the sections are the same size. One section may be juicier, and another may have more seeds. When peeling my tangerine, I spread each piece neatly and evenly on my saucer (that's my OCD kicking in—LOL). Although my tangerine is in separate pieces, it is still a whole piece of fruit.

I am sure you know where I am going with this. The apostle Paul in Galatians 5:22–23 reminds us about the *fruit of the spirit*. And though several attributes are listed, they all belong to the same whole fruit. Love is listed first as the covering. The internal organs are joy, peace, long-suffering, kindness, goodness, faithfulness, gentleness, and self-control. I am excited about this fruit.

For the most part, each section of the tangerine is orange, and basically all of the sections taste the same. The tangerine begins as a seed. It is planted, and watered. If it has the proper growing conditions, a tree grows, and tangerines are produced. Don't give me one of those fruits called Cuties, because they are not tangerines, nor are they oranges. They are a genetically modified organism (GMO). These foods are changed at the gene level and sometimes referred to as genetically engineered, genetically altered, or genetically manipulated.[15] This fruit is an imitation. It looks like, tastes like, and feels like the real thing but its attributes are not the same. Long term use of GMO foods may end up harming our bodies. We don't yet know.

We in the body of Christ must make sure that the spiritual fruit we seek is of God and *not* an imitation. The

---

15. *Encyclopedia Britannica*, online edition, *s.v.* "Genetically Modified Organism (GMO)."

words altered, engineered, and manipulated are words that describe what is in danger of happening, and has happened in some circles, to the message of Jesus Christ. His gospel is in danger of being a GMO. Christians must adhere to the same growing process as the tangerine. The first step is to accept God as your Father, and Jesus Christ as His Son and your Savior. This corresponds to the planting of the seed. As we develop and grow in the knowledge and the grace of God, we begin to exhibit the spiritual attributes and characteristics of God's garden.

> We in the body of Christ must make sure that the spiritual fruit we seek is of God and *not* an imitation. The words altered, engineered, and manipulated are words that describe what is in danger of happening, and has happened in some circles, to the message of Jesus Christ. His gospel is in danger of being a GMO.

As we consider fruit's spiritual attributes, love is listed first. Just as the outside of the fruit bears the burden of whatever is going on in the inside, so love acts as a covering and protection. Successful multicultural ministry, as does any successful ministry, begins with love. This empowers the ministry to flourish and exhibit the other attributes of the fruit. Cultivating this spiritual fruit means you are developing *a spirit like Christ's.*

Some may be of the persuasion that they need to travel outside the scope of Christian principles to successfully minister in a multicultural or urban environment, however this is not the case. It is staying and adhering to the spiritual bonds of love that Christ has already demonstrated for us that will allow your ministry to flourish.

Teaching and spreading love is the foundation of reconciliation. *Without love reconciliation is impossible.* Reconciling the masses without love is doomed to failure. Where does love begin? It begins with Christ in you. Love must be demonstrated daily and be unconditional. Undergirding every ministry is love. Jesus understood this when he gave the directive of the greatest commandment:

> And Jesus answered him, "The first of all the commandments is, Hear, O Israel; The Lord our God is one Lord: And thou shalt love the Lord thy God with all thy heart, and with all thy soul, and with all thy mind, and with all thy strength: this is the first commandment. And the second is like, namely this, Thou shalt love thy neighbour as thyself. There is none other commandment greater than these."
>
> (Mark 12:29–31)

In my humble opinion, we don't remind our churches, or ourselves, enough about this command and the attributes of love. Matthew 7:20 states, *"Wherefore by their fruits ye shall know them."* Let us desire to be known by our love.

Paul also understood the power and compassion of love when he said,

> I may be able to speak several foreign languages, and even the heavenly language of tongues, but if it is without love my words are incoherent and no one understands them. Even if I am an eloquent speaker or preacher, and can dissect the mysteries of the gospel, if I do it without love I am as an empty vessel. Even though it is a blessing to give above receiving, or be willing to die as a hero, these acts without love add nothing to my spiritual bank account: I am considered bankrupt! (1 Corinthians 13:1–3, my own paraphrase)

> *Love does not give up. Love is kind. Love is not jealous. Love does not put itself up as being important. Love has no pride. Love does not do the wrong thing. Love never thinks of itself. Love does not get angry. Love does not remember the suffering that comes from being hurt by someone. Love is not happy with sin. Love is happy with the truth. Love takes everything*

that comes without giving up. Love believes all things. Love hopes for all things. Love keeps on in all things. Love never comes to an end. ...And now we have these three: faith and hope and love, but the greatest of these is love. (1 Corinthians 13:4–8, 13 NLV)

Many are familiar with this text in the Bible. It is often read at weddings. The sound is poetic; these verses are highly spoken of in the literary community as a refined work. But these words are so much more than that. Love is the key to all the other spiritual fruit attributes. Until love has blossomed in our hearts, how can the other characteristics come to fruition? God's fruit is a spiritual matter. It is received through the Holy Spirit. Jesus said, *"That whatsoever ye shall ask of the Father in my name, he may give it you"* (John 15:16). Have you asked for your basket of love? Open wide your heart. He will give it to you.

Love is the key to all the other spiritual fruit attributes. Until love has blossomed in our hearts, how can the other characteristics come to fruition? God's fruit is a spiritual matter. It is received through the Holy Spirit.

A familiar saying we have in the church community is, "This joy that I have, the world didn't give it to me, and the world can't take it away!" When considering the joy-fruit, its attributes far exceed the feeling of being happy. Joy is a deep emotional characteristic. Joy is not manufactured, cannot be practiced, nor can it be taught. Joy is an attribute that runs through our minds like a river—it is ever flowing. The light of the joy-fruit may not always be at 150 watts, but it never goes out. You never need to wonder if this fruit is present in someone's heart, because it cannot be hidden. Joy keeps you strong. Nehemiah 8:10 says, *"Neither be ye sorry; for the joy of the LORD is your strength."* Joy keeps you in God's presence and keeps His presence in you. Psalm 16:11 says, *"In thy presence is fulness of joy; at thy right hand there are pleasures for evermore."*

No one can take your joy from you. Jesus assured us, *"These things have I spoken unto you, that my joy might remain in you, and that your joy might be full"* (John 15:11). *And ye now therefore have sorrow: but I will see you again, and your heart shall rejoice, and your joy no man taketh from you"* (John 16:22).

We understand that our gifts are given to us by God, but these spiritual fruits are different and must be developed. As leaders we must build a roadmap for those the Lord gives us to shepherd. There may be additional challenges when ministering to a multicultural group as we must be cognizant of the cultural differences. As the spiritual fruit of joy, peace, and patience are developed, ministries will become more cohesive and less divisive.

As leaders, ministers, and anyone faithful to the cause of Christ, we are all in. It is a huge heart commitment.

Take the story of the pig, the cow, and the hen. Lying on the breakfast table for their owners to eat are milk, eggs, cheese, bacon, and ham. The pig, cow, and hen are having a conversation between themselves about their contribution to the meal on the table. The cow said that he was disturbed early in the morning, because he had to provide the cream for the milk *and* the cheese. The chicken remarked that she had a hard time making her delivery that morning. Her labor was several minutes, and the last egg just took its time! Lastly, the pig chimed in and said, "I don't understand what you guys are complaining about. Ms. Cow, you can make some more cream tomorrow, and Ms. Chicken you can always lay another egg. But my brother, Willy, is not here anymore. He had to die to give that ham and bacon!"

We are Willy. We are the committed ones. The fruit that has developed in us, we demonstrate every day. Are we perfect? God forbid! We are but mere men traveling on the road to reconciliation ourselves, but we have an amazing calling to be an example to the body of Christ. "*The fruit of the righteous is a tree of life*" (Proverbs 11:30). "*And how can anyone preach unless they are sent? As it is written:*

'How beautiful are the feet of those who bring good news'"
(Romans 10:15–16 NIV).

Under the special covering of love, we continue developing as we seek the proper spiritual nutrition, which include all facets of the fruit of the spirit. The key—God uses ordinary people like you and me to do extraordinary things. We are fully equipped to break apart and break down every barrier. Multicultural ministry is first and foremost *ministry*. We would like to think there is some special formula to minister to those that we consider different from us. But it is our differences that make us uniquely lovable. As we embrace Christ we embrace one another.

8

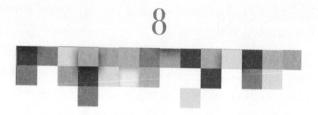

WHAT DOES LOVE HAVE
TO DO WITH IT?

I understand that we have already discussed the attribute of love as a critical component of the spiritual fruit in the previous chapter. However, the topic of love as it relates to multicultural and urban ministry must be dissected even further. Love is simple yet complex and encompasses many aspects. Love in the family unit is different from love in a romantic relationship. Love expressed in friendship is different from both of these.

Love is often conditional and contingent upon specific actions and expressions. Love is fickle, especially in romantic relationships. When you *fall in* love, you can often *fall out* of love just as easily. As siblings reach adulthood, it is sad to say, for various reasons, they can lose love toward one another and even toward their parents. As deep as familial love is, deeper still is hate.

Deon Jackson recorded a song in 1965. One of the lines says, "Love makes the world go around." There are many studies which directly relate love to the mental health of young children. God has wired us to give and received love. When love is not present, life is empty, and there is an undeniable void.

> God has wired us to give and received love.
> When love is not present, life is empty,
> and there is an undeniable void.

I am compelled to spend a moment on the ultimate love sacrifice of God our Father who gave Himself to save our lives. When we sit down and think about it we may ask, "Why? What prompted Him who is supreme to act so unselfishly on our behalf?" The answer is because of his love for us. He loved us in a way we may not truly understand or comprehend. But nevertheless, He left His ultimate example as a roadmap of how we as Christians should love. Philippians 2:5 directs us to have the mind of Christ. Later in the same chapter, the writer tells us that though He is God, for us He becomes our servant. Jesus fulfills His Father's love for us through His death. Only He could do that because He is perfectly sinless. Isn't that awesome! Who would do that? This is the type of love God desires for his children to have between one another. Imagine this kind of love in the hearts of God's children today. The church could change the world!

Can multiculturalism in ministry be as colorblind as God's love for us is? This love thing is gigantic, and it should be. As leaders we must always be moving in the direction of love. This should never become dull or out of focus in the ministry of reconciliation. The law of nature is that love begets love. What types of love are we talking about in regards to moving forward as a church body? There are specific definitions of love from the ancient Greek language.

Philia:(φιλία – philía) is love between friends.

Storge (στοργή – storgē) is affection felt by parents for their children.

Éros: (ἔρως – érōs) is intimate, passionate love or love experienced in romantic relationships.

Agape: (ἀγάπη – agape) is unconditional selfless, self-giving, sacrificial love.

The love for healing differences between ethnicities is agape love. This love says that no matter our past, our differences, our individualities, or our destinies, we love you! Have you ever told someone you love them, and they said they love you back? It's wonderful!

The most difficult challenge is teaching people how to love unconditionally. The first step is to demonstrate love to them through our actions. The second step is directing them to the Word so they may catch the infilling of the Holy Spirit is God's divine prescription. And we all know that only Christ can change a person's heart. We must let others know that we have gone through spiritual heart surgery. Christ's love is manifest in us. The love seed is planted, and we are growing it as mustard seeds. Hallelujah!

9

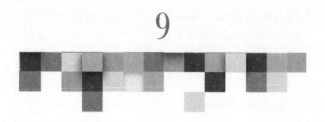

BRINGING THE INJURED

How can the church hide from what is going on in our society? In a city like Chicago, on any given weekend it is probable and possible that a black teenager will lose his or her life. Similar incidents are happening in the Hispanic community as well. This is a real and in-your-face issue.

As we look at the poor in this country, we know theirs is an uphill battle. Even as we consider middle-class families, often these folks are living from paycheck to paycheck and carry the financial and often emotional burden of extended family members. I remember one of my members telling me that a vice president at the corporation she worked for wanted to know her favorite charity. She told me she wanted to say, "My family!"

Each person must view another through the eyes of humanity. First and foremost, we are human. We are uniquely made. God made us a little lower than the angels. Look at this song in Psalm 8:3–8:

> When I consider your heavens, the work of your fingers, the moon and the stars, which you have set in place, what is mankind that you are mindful of them, human beings that you care for them? You have made them a little lower than the angels and crowned them with glory and honor. You made them rulers over the works of your hands; you put everything under their feet: all flocks and herds, and the animals of the wild, the birds in the sky, and the fish in the sea, all that swim the paths of the seas.   (NIV)

Critical in understanding humanity is to master the *art of observance*, in partnership with the *art of listening*. An astute observer who can see without prejudice, without preconceptions, and with the ability to see beyond the obvious, will be a blessing to the people of God. This type of observation is a spiritual act of worship. It yields a special anointing that opens your heart to an eclectic mixture of God's precious people. To observe incorporates discernment.

An astute observer who can see without prejudice, without preconceptions, and with the ability to see beyond the obvious, will be a blessing to the people of God. This type of observation is a spiritual act of worship. It yields a special anointing that opens your heart to an eclectic mixture of God's precious people.

It takes getting involved with people by not only observing who they are, but also by listening to what people are saying. This kind of listening is also a spiritual act of worship. You listen for more than obtaining information, but for how to best serve and minister to them effectively. Observing and listening in this capacity helps to develop a compassionate heart, so needed in ministry.

Another component to understanding humanity is being in *alignment*. This means to be in a correct position, including making adjustments as needed. Many stores sell blood pressure monitors if you want to check your blood pressure at home. Sometimes the home machines do not register appropriately because they need to be returned to the manufacturer to be recalibrated. Once the machine is recalibrated, it is back in alignment and can be used accurately. Right positioning, lining up in accordance with your church's vision, situating your spiritual outlook in accordance with the perfect will of our Father, and willingness to follow the vision set before you, are successful ingredients.

Multicultural ministry is not a one man show. You cannot do everything and be everything to everybody as your ministry grows. I endeavor to equip Lighthouse Church with one hundred middle-door pastors. In fact we have both elders and pastors at Lighthouse. These men and women of God have gone through training at the All Nations Leadership Institute (ANLI). At ANLI we have courses specifically designed to train our students in multicultural leadership in addition to regular biblical studies. ANLI is one of the methods used in recruiting those with a heart to minister multiculturally. The training at ANLI is not only academic, but also hands-on. We believe in training by doing. *"Faith without works is dead"* (James 2:26). The need to recruit workers in the ministry, as every leader knows, is an ongoing process. I believe as you go forth, God will give you discernment and insight into the heart of specific people whom God has equipped for specific ministries.

These tools drive man's humanity to man. No matter what people believe, whether they are Christian, from a non-Christian religion, agnostic, or atheist, they must acknowledge humanity and the equality of being human. A rule of thumb is the golden rule, simply to treat others as you desire to be treated. It's unfortunate that something so simple is so difficult for people to emulate. In my mind, humanity means to be humane. We are to be caring, kind, and compassionate to each other. We are to promote respect, peace, and harmony among ourselves.

A rule of thumb is the golden rule, simply to treat others as you desire to be treated. It's unfortunate that something so simple is so difficult for people to emulate. In my mind, humanity means to be humane. We are to be caring, kind, and compassionate to each other. We are to promote respect, peace, and harmony among ourselves.

We are inhumane when we treat others differently for no reason other than historical hypocrisy and injustices based on themes of irrational prejudices. I am aware that some of the roadblocks to unify humanity in this country are at times overwhelming. We have only to look at the current political climate we face in America today. However, Christ clothed himself in humanity to save us. He did this not only for the purpose of salvation, but also to put himself in our shoes. Christ, through His Father's indwelling power, is without sin. He was totally human. Since Christ's power resides in us, we too have the divine power to walk in our full humanity. God is not calling for a powerless church to stand idly by and minister in a vacuum. His desire is that humanity be our lifestyle.

10

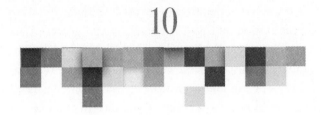

EMPOWERING TO SERVE

One of the keys to empowering leaders and workers in multicultural ministry is to do so through initiating them to action. This means getting folks involved in community events, learning opportunities, counseling, and social activities. For several years in the summer, Lighthouse has sponsored an outreach event we call Soul Patrol. We have so much fun as we go out spreading the gospel of Jesus Christ by meaningfully ministering to the physical, tangible, and spiritual needs of our community.

One of our activities is to set up at the local food store and gas station and give out free gas and groceries over a two-hour period. More than one hundred Lighthouse members volunteer once a week over an eight-week period to carry out random acts of kindness to our neighbors. What could be a better way of empowering people than to give them the opportunity for selfless giving? Not only does this foster bonding with one another, but it shows the community multicultural ministry in action. How powerful is that? In John 5:19, Jesus said, *"Truly, truly, I say to you, the Son can do nothing of his own accord, but only what he sees the Father doing. For whatever the Father does, that the Son does likewise"* (esv). Just as Jesus' earthly actions reflected God's love and ministry, your community will mirror your love and ministry in their actions.

Another powerful vision God placed in my heart is to not only take multicultural ministry to the community but to also take it to believers within a ten mile radius of Lighthouse. God placed the Lighthouse Church building on a street that runs ten miles east and west. Over the years, I endeavored to contact every church pastor located to the east and to the west of Lighthouse for an annual Thanksgiving service. We call it "Miracle on 127th Street." What an exponential blessing this has grown to be. It just blows my socks off to see fellow pastors and their members united together under one roof. We are singing together, dancing together, praying together—all colors, all ethnicities, and all denominations—what rejoicing! Hallelujah! What God wants us to do is catapult out of that box of mediocrity to implement the ideas he has birthed inside all of us.[16] These are only a couple of the many things we implement to empower folks through action.

> What God wants us to do is catapult out of that box of mediocrity to implement the ideas he has birthed inside all of us.

To empower others is to encourage them. This can be done with compliments, acknowledgements, inclusion, thoughtfulness, and the list goes on. Proverbs 12:25 says, *"Anxiety in a man's heart weighs him down, but a good word makes him glad"* (ESV). Empowering others also empowers you. Help empower others by incorporating recruiting, training, and action with good works.

---

16. See the biography page at the end of the book for contact information Pastor Dan Willis if you need information on how to implement these programs and others.

11

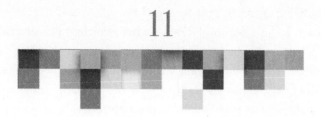

OUR CALLING

When considering a focus to lead multiculturally, ministry in this area must be a calling because of its complexities. In this country race remains a complicated and difficult subject. As the backdrop of America changes and people of different ethnicities intermarry resulting in cultures blending, ministry in this area becomes even more relevant. God gave me the heart to want to bring *all* people together. For me *separatism* in worship is quite unnatural. I endeavor to make Sunday morning worship ethnically diverse, one service at a time.

As the backdrop of America changes and people of different ethnicities intermarry resulting in cultures blending, ministry in this area becomes even more relevant. God gave me the heart to want to bring *all* people together. For me *separatism* in worship is quite unnatural.

I am thrilled to say that all over America churches *are* making inroads toward multicultural ministry. This is so exciting! In 2012, the Grace Church Roseville, located in Minnesota, hosted their "Coming Together Conference." Dr. Mark DeYmaz, the keynote speaker, presented a seminar using the title of a book he wrote, *Building a Healthy Multi-Ethnic Church*. I bring up this seminar as it is representative of some of the attributes I have discussed in this text. Tony Evans published the book *Oneness Embraced* in 2011, in which he takes an in-depth look at reconciliation, the kingdom, and justice. I mention these books as resources among the growing number of theologians delving into this critical ministry area. Obviously, more are seeing the need to bring God's people together as one body in Christ.

However, there is still a mountain of work to do, a number of bridges to cross in order to get to where we need to be. I refuse to be naïve about the challenges of those who have the heart and the calling to mend the broken fences of racial reconciliation. It is very interesting that in this country, we work at the same companies, we shop at the same grocery stores, and our children attend some of the same schools, yet on Sunday morning we worship with people who, for the most part, only look like us. However, if one can chase a thousand, and two can chase ten thousand through the power of God, we are well equipped for this battle. (See Deuteronomy 32:30–31.)

I have tried hopefully in a relatable way, to lay down some of the basics of multicultural ministry and how Christ has provided the foundation for its success. We have but to follow Him. The question becomes, *are we willing?* Jesus asks his disciples to go and make believers of all nations. (See Matthew 28:19.)

Whether taking the gospel locally or around the world, please consider *your manner* as you bring this message. We are evangelists and missionaries. If a nation, a person, or a group, is ignorant of the message of Christ, it does not make you better or higher than they are because you know His message. I love it when I find someone who is totally unchurched. They are often some of the best converts. They are unaware of church traditions and are free in their hearts to worship and absorb the things of God without preconceived restrictions. Hallelujah! It is a gift to have childlike faith regarding the things of God.

Sometimes we unintentionally make ministry complicated. To be honest, people are, on occasion, complicated, difficult, and irrational, and may impede progress at times. But through Christ we are overcomers. We are taught that no weapon formed against us believers shall prosper. (See Isaiah 54:17.)

If you are reading this book, then God has placed a seed in your heart for an uncompromising and unconditional ministry to *all* believers. Allow the pattern of love that Jesus has already designed to be your map on this journey to reconciliation. Go forth in your calling; nothing is sure except for His hope that is in you!

ABOUT THE AUTHOR

Dan Willis did not exactly envision a life in ministry as a young boy growing up in Chicago. Though he loved the contagious rhythms of gospel music, he never imagined that one day he'd be creating them himself. Yet from these humble beginnings developed one of today's leading pastors.

As a young boy, Dan's dreams involved entering the medical field as a neurosurgeon until the fateful day when, at age sixteen, he was called to "temporarily" take over as pastor of a local church. Dan is still there, serving as the